I0813165

DISCOVERING THE UNITED STATES

New York

BY IB LARSEN

Kids Core

An Imprint of Abdo Publishing
abdobooks.com

abdobooks.com

Published by Abdo Publishing, a division of ABDO, PO Box 398166, Minneapolis, Minnesota 55439.

Printed in China.
052024
092024

THIS BOOK CONTAINS RECYCLED MATERIALS

Cover Photo: Luciano Mortula/Shutterstock Images
Interior Photos: Amy Sancetta/AP Images, 4–5; Monitor Picture Library/Popperfoto/Getty Images, 6; Steve Byland/Shutterstock Images, 7 (top left); iStockphoto, 7 (top right), 7 (bottom right), 9, 28 (top right); Anzhela Shvab/Shutterstock Images, 7 (bottom left); Matt Champlin/Moment/Getty Images, 10; Vespasian/Alamy, 12–13; Universal History Archive/Universal Images Group/Getty Images, 15; Shutterstock Images, 17; Chokkicx/DigitalVision Vectors/Getty Images, 18; Sean Pavone/iStockphoto, 20–21; Pandora Pictures/Shutterstock Images, 22; Colin D. Young/Shutterstock Images, 23; Sergii Figurnyi/Shutterstock Images, 24, 26; Red Line Editorial, 28 (left), 29; Tom Till/Alamy, 28 (middle right); Tada Images/Shutterstock Images, 28 (bottom right)

Editor: Christa Kelly
Series Designer: Katharine Hale

Library of Congress Control Number: 2023949361

Publisher's Cataloging-in-Publication Data

Names: Larsen, Ib, author.
Title: New York / by Ib Larsen
Description: Minneapolis, Minnesota: Abdo Publishing, 2025 | Series: Discovering the United States | Includes online resources and index.
Identifiers: ISBN 9781098294021 (lib. bdg.) | ISBN 9798384913290 (ebook)
Subjects: LCSH: U.S. states--Juvenile literature. | New York (State)--History--Juvenile literature. | Northeastern States--Juvenile literature. | Physical geography--United States--Juvenile literature.
Classification: DDC 973--dc23

All population data taken from:
"Estimates of Population by Sex, Race, and Hispanic Origin: April 1, 2020 to July 1, 2022." *US Census Bureau, Population Division*, June 2023, census.gov.

CONTENTS

Several Woodstock music festivals have been held in the decades since the original event.

CHAPTER 1

Woodstock

It was the morning of August 18, 1969. About 40,000 people were gathered on a farm in Bethel, New York, for a rock music festival. The festival was called Woodstock. Some people watched from picnic blankets. Others stood by the stage.

Jimi Hendrix was a singer and guitarist. He was born in 1942 in Seattle, Washington.

After three days of music, it was the last day of the festival.

Most people had already left. But those who remained would see one of rock's most famous performances. Jimi Hendrix and his band were about to take the stage.

Hendrix played some of his most popular songs. The crowd clapped, sang along, and danced. Near the end of his time on stage, Hendrix played a version of

New York Facts

DATE OF STATEHOOD
July 26, 1788

CAPITAL
Albany

POPULATION
19,677,151

AREA
54,555 square miles
(141,297 sq km)

STATE BIRD

Eastern bluebird

STATE TREE

Sugar maple

STATE FLOWER

Rose

STATE MAMMAL

American beaver

Each US state has a different population, size, and capital city. States also have state symbols.

"The Star-Spangled Banner." Hendrix was already famous before Woodstock. But his performance there made him legendary. Today, the festival is an important part of US history.

New York's Land

New York is in the Northeast region of the United States. Canada borders the state to the north and west. Pennsylvania and New Jersey border New York to the south. Vermont, Massachusetts, and Connecticut lie to the east.

New York has mountains, valleys, hills, and plains. The state also has many bodies of water. A small part of southeastern New York borders

New York's Mountains

New York has several mountain ranges. The Adirondack Mountains are in northeastern New York. Maple, birch, and beech trees cover the mountain range. In the southeast are the Catskill Mountains. Bobcats and black bears call the Catskills home.

The number of humpback whales off the coast of New York is increasing.

the Atlantic Ocean. Humpback whales feed near the shore. Western New York borders Lake Ontario and Lake Erie, two of the largest lakes in the country.

Lake Ontario's name comes from an Iroquois word meaning "beautiful lake."

New York has cold, snowy winters. The land near Lake Ontario and Lake Erie gets extra snow. New York's summers are warm and **humid**. Summers are hotter in the cities because concrete traps heat from the sun. Autumns and springs bring pleasant temperatures.

Further Evidence

Look at the website below. Does it give any new evidence to support Chapter One?

New York

abdocorelibrary.com/discovering-new-york

More than 81,000 Iroquois people live in the United States.

The People of New York

American Indians first came to New York about 13,000 years ago. Many nations called the land home, including the Mohicans, Munsees, and Iroquois. Early Iroquois people farmed corn and beans. They also hunted and fished.

The Iroquois lived in **longhouses** that held several related families.

In the 1600s, white **settlers** arrived from the Netherlands. Great Britain seized the land in 1669. After the Revolutionary War (1775–1783), New York became a US state.

Many people who **immigrated** to the United States first arrived in New York. In the late 1800s and early 1900s, New York Harbor

Ellis Island

Ellis Island is off the coast of New York City. In the late 1800s and early 1900s, millions of immigrants entered the United States through Ellis Island. The island now hosts a museum where visitors can learn about what life was like for early immigrants.

Most of the immigrants who arrived at Ellis Island came from Europe.

was the busiest immigration site in the country. People came to New York from countries around the world.

Today, 54 percent of people in New York are white. Almost 20 percent are Hispanic or Latino. About 18 percent are Black. Almost 10 percent are Asian, and 1 percent are American Indian.

Many famous people come from New York. Actor Timothée Chalamet is from the state.

So is basketball player Michael Jordan. Five US presidents were also from New York.

Culture

New York is famous for its food. New York pizza comes in wide slices on a thin crust. New York bagels are also popular. They're boiled before baking to soften the bread. Pastrami-on-rye sandwiches are popular among New York's Jewish population. The sandwich was invented in New York City in 1888.

Music is another important part of New York's culture. New York City is known as the birthplace of hip-hop. Artists began practicing hip-hop in New York City in the 1970s. Hip-hop involves rapping, dancing, and **deejaying**.

Italian immigrants were the first people to sell pizza in New York.

Today, hip-hop is one of the most popular kinds of music in the United States.

Sports are also important in New York. The state has three professional football teams. It also has two professional baseball teams and three professional basketball teams.

The word *Excelsior* is New York's state motto. It means "ever upward."

Industries

New York is known for its **financial** industry. Many people in the state are bankers. Others work with the **stock market**.

Other people in New York work in journalism. The *New York Times* and the *Wall Street Journal*, two of the country's most popular newspapers, are based in the state. The state also has many book publishing companies.

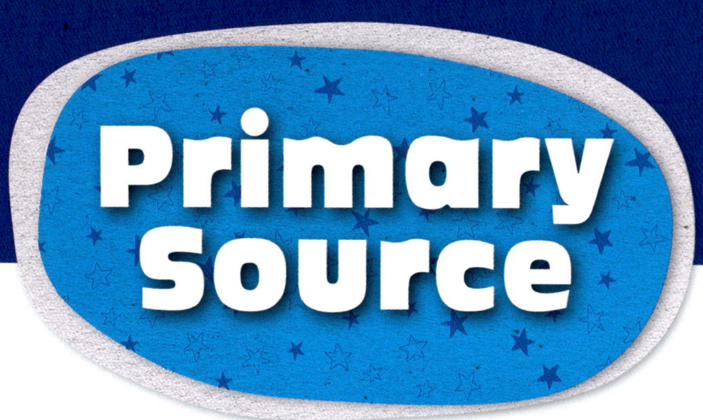

Photographer Nick Johnson explained why New York pizza is so special:

> It's comfort food. It's meant to be shared. It's food for celebrating and for feeling down. It's the food of the people.

Source: Daniel Schwartz. "A Slice of Old-School New York: The Photo Project That Puts Pizza Parlors First." *Fathom*, fathomaway.com, 30 Aug. 2017. Accessed 9 Oct. 2023.

What's the Big Idea?

Read this quote carefully. What is its main idea? Explain how the main idea is supported by details.

Albany became New York's capital in 1797.

CHAPTER 3

Places in New York

Albany is the capital of New York. It is located in the eastern portion of the state. The city has history museums and art museums.

New York City is located in southern New York. It is the country's most **populated** city. It is home to 8 million people.

More than 42 million people visit Central Park every year.

The city is separated into five areas called boroughs. The boroughs are the Bronx, Brooklyn, Manhattan, Queens, and Staten Island.

New York City borders the Atlantic Ocean. One of the most famous places in the city is Central Park. It is an 843-acre (341-ha) park on the island of Manhattan. It has a zoo, an ice-skating rink, and playgrounds. The park also has an art museum and a castle.

Adirondack Park covers almost one-fifth of New York.

Parks and Nature

New York has many parks. Adirondack Park is one of the most famous. This park is located in northern New York. It protects 6 million acres (2.4 million ha) of the Adirondack Mountains. Visitors can fish in the park's lakes and hike on its trails. They can also visit the Wild Center.

Niagara Falls State Park is the country's oldest state park.

There, visitors can learn about the plants and animals that live in the park.

People in New York can also visit the Appalachian National Scenic Trail. This long hiking route follows the Appalachian Mountains.

It runs from Maine to Georgia and passes through the southern part of New York. Few people walk the trail's full length. It takes months to hike from one end of the trail to the other.

Landmarks

Niagara Falls is one of New York's most famous landmarks. It is also sacred to the Iroquois people. The falls are made up of three waterfalls on the Niagara River. The river separates New York from Canada.

Annie Edson Taylor

On October 24, 1901, 63-year-old Annie Edson Taylor went over Niagara Falls. She rode down the falls in a padded barrel. She survived with only a small cut on her forehead.

The Statue of Liberty was designed by French sculptor Frédéric Auguste Bartholdi.

Many people visit New York to take a boat tour to the base of the falls.

The Statue of Liberty is another important landmark. It is located off the coast of New York City. It stands 305 feet (93 m) tall. France gave the statue to the United States in the 1800s.

It is now one of the United States' most famous symbols.

New York is a land of opportunity. People who want a big-city experience can visit New York City. Those seeking nature can explore the state's parks. And people who want to try new food can have a slice of the state's famous pizza. New York has something for everyone.

Explore Online

Visit the website below. What new information did you learn about the Appalachian National Scenic Trail that wasn't in Chapter Three?

Appalachian National Scenic Trail

abdocorelibrary.com/discovering-new-york

State Map

KEY

Capital

Park

City or town

Point of interest

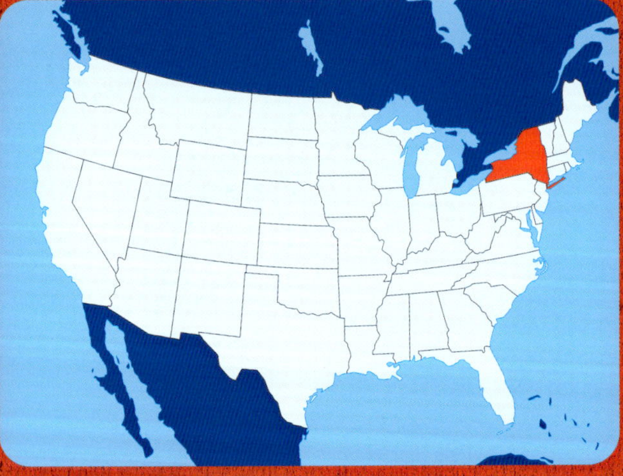

Catskill Mountains

Adirondack Park

New York Times Building

New York: The Empire State

Glossary

deejaying
playing recorded music while adding new effects in real time

financial
relating to money

humid
describing air that has a lot of moisture

immigrated
moved to another country

longhouses
long, low, one-room buildings made of wood and bark

populated
settled or lived in

settlers
people who moved to a new area

stock market
the market of buying and selling portions of companies

Online Resources

To learn more about New York, visit our free resource websites below.

Visit **abdocorelibrary.com** or scan this QR code for free Common Core resources for teachers and students, including vetted activities, multimedia, and booklinks, for deeper subject comprehension.

Visit **abdobooklinks.com** or scan this QR code for free additional online weblinks for further learning. These links are routinely monitored and updated to provide the most current information available.

Learn More

Berne, Emma Carlson. *The History of the American Revolution*. Rockridge Press, 2021.

Hewson, Anthony K. *New York Yankees*. Abdo, 2023.

Murray, Julie. *New York*. Abdo, 2020.

Index

About the Author

Ib Larsen is a writer and editorial assistant living in Saint Paul, Minnesota.